Seals

Words to practise

seals sea beach

eat each teach

Seals swim in the sea. Seals eat fish.

The seals swim to a beach.

The seals go up to the top of the beach.

The seals have a pup each on the beach.

The seal pups are big. The pups go to the sea.

The seal pups have fun in the sea.

The seals teach the pups to catch fish.